# After the Honeymoon

## How to Have a Gratifying Retirement

VIRGIL L. BRADY

## AFTER THE HONEYMOON
## HOW TO HAVE A GRATIFYING RETIREMENT

Scripture quotations marked NRSV are taken from the New Revised Standard Version of the Bible, Copyright © 1989, by the Division of Christian Education of the National Council of the Churches of Christ in the United States of America. Used by permission. All rights reserved. Website

iUniverse books may be ordered through booksellers or by contacting:

iUniverse
1663 Liberty Drive
Bloomington, IN 47403
www.iuniverse.com
1-800-Authors (1-800-288-4677)

ISBN: 978-1-5320-6958-1 (sc)
ISBN: 978-1-5320-6959-8 (e)

Library of Congress Control Number: 2019902270

Print information available on the last page.

iUniverse rev. date: 02/25/2019

# Contents

# *Introduction*

After nineteen years, I am still learning how to retire. I have read most of the books on retirement. I find there no prescription. A gratifying retirement is the result of a process. Continual and honest examination of our individual personality is the key. Accepting this reality has helped me enjoy the process. I invite you to join me in this exciting and challenging journey.

I have not always practiced what I preached. I have always believed what I preached. Understanding how my unique personality shapes retirement has not always been a simple task. It is a process worthy of serious consideration. I believe this book will help your retirement to be a gratifying experience, and you will enjoy the ride.

# One

## The Fundamentals of Retirement

How to have a gratifying retirement. How YOU can have a gratifying retirement.

Notice the difference between these two sentences. The second one contains the word "you". The focus of this book will be on how YOU can have a gratifying retirement.

Each of us bleeds the same color, and yet we are very different. Each of us has our distinct personality. We are complex individuals. The degree of our neurosis and insecurities varies from person to person. Individual personality characteristics affect many decisions made during retirement. Each person needs to do retirement in a way that fits for them.

For retirement to be a positive and growing experience, start by embracing these four words: Difficult, Different, Work, Enjoyable.

1. Retirement is difficult. You may respond to this statement by saying, "What do you mean, difficult? What can be difficult about being free of responsibility? How can retirement be difficult without the pressure of going to work every morning?"

To say that retirement is difficult is not a negative statement. Scott Peck begins his classic bestseller, *The Road Less Traveled*, with this sentence: "Life is difficult." Peck continues: "This is a great truth because once we truly see this truth, we transcend it. Once we truly know that life is difficult— once we truly understand and accept it—then life is no longer difficult... What makes life difficult is that the process of confronting and solving problems is a painful one...Problems evoke in us frustration or grief or sadness or loneliness or guilt or fear or anxiety or anguish or despair... Yet it is in this whole process of meeting and solving problems that life

1

has its meaning…It is because of the problems that we grow mentally and spiritually…" (p.15, 16)

It will be incredibly important to reread this quote and insert the word "retirement" for "life". Peck goes to great length to point out how problems are increased when we try to avoid or ignore them.

In his book, *Retirement is not for sissises*, David McKenna understands that retirement is difficult. "With advancing years come the grim realities of declining energy, health, and memory. Even people of great faith and a growing spirit will agree that old age puts to test our grit and our grace… Retirement is a succession of shocks."

I wish someone had told me that retirement would be difficult. Understanding and accepting this fact would have helped me deal with the many retirement issues. One author said it takes two to three years to master the art of retirement. It is taking me seventeen years, and I am still learning new things about how to have a gratifying retirement. Writing this book is helping me. Hopefully, reading this book will help you accept that retirement is difficult, and thereby fully enjoy this phase of life.

2. Retirement is different. You may say that this is obvious. I confess I did not realize how different retirement is. Here are two of the many ways retirement is different.

First, we know that good things happen as a result of hard work. Throughout my career, I approached leisure as something to be earned. Working hard in my occupation increased my permission to enjoy leisure time. In retirement, leisure is no longer time that is earned. The feelings that accompany _unearned_ leisure time are quite different.

Second, your date book will look different. I vividly remember my first day of retirement. I woke up at the same time, shaved, showered, dressed and ate breakfast. Then it hit me as I opened my date book. There was nothing—blank. My date book was always filled with tasks to be completed. Some of those tasks were my decision. Many were merely requirements and expectations of the job.

In retirement, we may have a date book, but now it is filled with what we decide to do with our leisure. It is different getting up every morning without a schedule already set. In retirement, we transition from ongoing activities and a schedule to a non-scheduled approach to life. Often we are not prepared for it to happen so quickly.

Steve Harper in his book, *Stepping Aside, Moving Ahead* talks about how we are "patterned to keep multiple plates spinning at once." Then we come face to face with the abundant amount of free/leisure time. It is definitely different and can be difficult.

3. Retirement is work. Harper writes: "One of the details is facing the fact that retiring is hard work." McKenna captures this reality: "I confess that I was not prepared for retirement to require so much work. Once I accepted this fact, I began to relax and enter into the work of retirement with a new attitude."

Throughout our career, most of us gave ourselves to improving. We were determined to remain vital and growing. This was a process that helped avoid becoming stale and burned out. Our continuing education included reading, seminars and prayer. Applying the same discipline/work throughout our retirement years will keep a person vital and growing.

4. Retirement is enjoyable when we accept that retirement is difficult, different and work. Understanding and embracing these four concepts will serve as emotional and spiritual power for retirement years.

Like most retirees, over the years, I went through several stages. One stage was the honeymoon stage. The first several months were new, novel and exciting. Then the realities and issues that must be faced in retirement hit me like a brick. The novel and new began to wear off. I was face to face with some thoughts and feelings that were not experienced during the honeymoon phase.

Like many pastors, I did my share of pre-marital counseling. I served a church in a university town. The church building had a long center aisle and the largest pipe organ in the state of Kansas. Many young couples from the community and university chose our sanctuary for their wedding.

I invited (required) couples to visit with me for two sessions of pre-marital consultation. Most of the couples, especially the younger ones, were just going through the motions, fulfilling a requirement.

One question I always ask couples is: When you get angry with each other, what do you do or not do, say or not say? What is your pattern when you have an argument? Inevitably, they looked at me with a blank expression and then responded: "Oh, we don't get angry with each other. We may have a few disagreements, but we work it out." I tried my best to avoid saying: "You are so naïve."

After four years of marriage, a husband phoned me. He said, "Remember when you asked us about our anger and I said we don't get angry. Well, today I saw my wife's anger and boy was it a whopper. I think we need to revisit your suggestions on how to deal with anger in a marriage." For this couple, the honeymoon lasted about four years. For many couples, it lasts for less time.

In the retirement workshop I conduct, sometimes a person responds with a blank look as if to say, "This does not apply to me." For new retirees, the honeymoon may last for two days, or two years or ten years. When the honeymoon is over, we begin to seriously address the difficult and different issues that confront all of us who are retired.

I asked Randal and Joan how they responded to the six issues I presented during my retirement workshop. By their response and facial expressions, I got the impression they did not fully grasp the implications of each idea that I offered. They were excited about being retired. They had great expectations. Like a young couple coming for pre-marital counseling, they were not ready to examine the complexities and realities of retirement. Randal and Joan may need to be retired for a while before they are ready to examine the key issue that faces all of us in retirement.

After fifteen years of retirement, something different began to happen within me. To my amazement, I was still in one of the honeymoon phases of my retirement. I entered a new and different period of retirement and began dealing with issues that I had not experience before.

For fifteen years I played golf almost every day. I wrote four books. Elaine and I traveled abroad and throughout the states. We continued to live in the town where I worked for fifteen years. This provided me a few opportunities to contribute the gifts I had given for the 38 years of my career. My identity remained in place. Three months out of the year we drove across country to stay near our three children and seven grandchildren.

All of a sudden I realized that I had been in a honeymoon phase of retirement. This happened when we moved from Kansas to California. My interest in playing lots of golf began to wane. I did not have any more ideas for another book. Our travel-bucket list was nearly empty. No one knew what I did for 38 years. When they found out, they didn't care. We saw our kids and grandchildren several times a week. Suddenly I had to rethink what it means to have a gratifying retirement.

Vivian related her story to me. "I enjoyed my retirement for twenty-five years, and then my health changed dramatically. I had difficulty walking, and I slowly became legally blind. When I heard you talking about the honeymoon phase of retirement, I realized my twenty-five years of retirement had been a honeymoon, at least compared to what I was experiencing now. The change has not been easy. Realizing I need to move past the honeymoon is helping me adjust."

I hope your retirement honeymoon lasts as long as you want and when it ends you will make the changes that make sense.

# Questions for Personal Reflection and Group Discussion

1. What is your response to inserting "retirement" in place of "life" in the Peck quotation?
2. Are you prepared for how different retirement can be? Why? Why not?
3. In what ways have you or will you _work_ at having a gratifying retirement?
4. Have there been or do you anticipate there will be times when retirement is not enjoyable? Why? Why not?
5. How does the honeymoon phase of retirement relate to your experience?

# Two

## Activate Your Power

Numerous books are available that offer suggestions on how to have a gratifying retirement. I googled, "How to have a successful retirement" and found a wealth of information. Because there is sufficient information about the financial and legal facets of retirement, this book will not address those issues. The focus of this book is the role of the mental, spiritual and emotional aspects of retirement.

Here is an abbreviated list of some ideas that various books on retirement offer for a gratifying retirement. You can find many more suggestions.

Adjust to change
Keep a sense of humor
Be creative
Take risks
Be flexible
Be open-minded
Have a healthy attitude
Be motivated
Put money in proper perspective
Create purpose and meaning
Create and maintain great friends
Plan
Find out what activities you are passionate about
Master the moment (live in the present)
Set goals

Learn how to use leisure
Continue to grow and feel alive
Inventory your interest
Embrace contradiction
Stay Healthy
Get a part-time job
Stay engaged
Plan your income
Learn new things
Master challenges
Build confidence in weak areas
Look for opportunities for personal growth, achievement and satisfaction
Seek out new opportunities to socialize.
List your 10 favorite interests and activities
The joy of Not Working: tons of ideas for activities

If these ideas on how to retire are relevant and helpful, use them to the fullest. However, I have seen, in myself and others, how implementing a useful suggestion is not easy. Just because someone has been given good advice does not mean the idea will become integrated into his/her retirement lifestyle.

Most of us have personality barriers, stoppers, obstacles that block us from accomplishing an idea even though we recognize it would be helpful. For example, have you resisted doing something that made sense because you were worried about what others would think? Have you ever wanted to try something but didn't because you were afraid you would mess it up or fail altogether? Has someone suggested a course of action but you stopped yourself from accomplishing it because of your fear of disappointing them? Have you wanted to change a part of your personality but resisted because it required too much energy and thought?

Here are the testimonies of several people who had difficulty taking a useful retirement suggestion and putting it into practice. They have mental and/or emotional barriers that kept them from applying a helpful suggestion.

Be Creative: Sue responded to this suggestion. "After a couple years of retirement, I found myself struggling. Someone suggested I needed to be more creative with my time. They pointed out that creativity opens a world of opportunities. I knew they were right, but found it difficult to put into action. I was a great wife and mother of five children. I was diligent. My ideas for raising children were what most good parents do, and I was good at it. But I never saw myself as creative. I am not sure why? I guess my insecurities about being creative got in my way. I seem to have mind-blockers when I begin thinking about being creative. Maybe I am afraid I will try to be creative and fail.

Adjust to Change: To this suggestion, Jack said: "My work did not require that I adjust to change. I think that is one of the reasons I liked my work and was good at it. I don't think I would have done well in a job that called for me to change from time to time. I have never liked too much change. I like things predictable. When a friend pointed out that the difficulty I was having in retirement was because I was slow to embrace change, well, that was not very helpful even though I knew he was right."

Find a Purpose: Joseph says: "I loved my job. I had a purpose for getting up each morning. Now, in retirement, I am having difficulty finding purpose in my use of time. What purpose is there in playing golf, reading, taking walks and doing projects around the house? People tell me that I need a higher purpose. For some reason, I have not found something that appeals to me. Believe me, I have received numerous suggestions from many people. All my life, my work gave me purpose and meaning."

Here is Max's story. "As I was learning to retire, I read a book that suggested an essential element of a gratifying retirement is seeking out new opportunities to socialize. I was told to cultivate a social network. My entire professional career was caring about and helping people. I was involved with people nearly eight hours a day. Cultivating a social network may be good advice for some, but it does not appeal to me in my retirement years. Because I worked so vigorously with people, I never learned how to be alone. You can see I am in a bind when it comes to my use of time in retirement."

After living in Kansas for 76 years, Elaine and I recently moved to southern California. Being close to our three children and seven grandchildren was a decision we both agreed was the right one. Shortly after we arrived, tension emerged in our relationship. We went to see a counselor. She listened and offered several suggestions. The suggestions were on target, but we resisted applying her ideas. Why? Each of us had thoughts and feelings that were blocking us from putting her ideas into practice. Moving was a death experience, which included feelings of fear, guilt, and anger. To activate the counselor's suggestions, we discovered the importance of identifying and examining the emotional barriers that were blocking us from doing what made sense.

Books on retirement offer useful suggestions. Some of the ideas are action related, and some have to do with attitude. These stories are just a sample of many illustrations of how we may come across a good suggestion for a healthy retirement, but certain thoughts and feelings block us from putting the idea into action.

I have discovered that my barriers are usually a feeling. Limiting the power of the barrier comes by identifying the feeling or feelings.

In response to the question what are you feeling, we often say we feel "bad" or "hurt". Worried, disappointed, anxious, depressed and upset are words that are frequently used to express a feeling. Consider four words that sum up all of these vulnerable feelings: guilt, fear, lonely and anger. I recommend you consider these four words when you want to name what is blocking you from implementing a good retirement suggestion. Guilt, fear, loneliness, and anger will sabotage our efforts to put into action an idea that we realize would be good for our emotional and mental health.

What are the barriers/feelings you have that stop you from implementing a good idea for retirement? What is the best way for dealing with the barriers? Here are three steps for answering this question.

First, name the barrier. Down through history, in literature, philosophy, and folklore, there have been those who advocate that giving a name to someone or an object means you have control or power over the named. Naming is a dynamic way to claim and own what is happening in us. This leads to a healthy attitude towards the experiences of life and to whatever the future holds.

I have a friend who invited me to an open meeting of Alcohol Anonymous. When he introduced himself he said, "My name is Jed, and I am an alcoholic." He proceeded to tell his story which included a divorce and lots of pain. After the meeting, I asked him why he introduced himself that way. He told me that each person chooses how they introduce themselves. I do it this way because it helps me own my disease. For many years I was in denial and blamed others. Forthrightly naming my illness has been a significant part of my recovery. For some reason, saying the words give me a sense of power. I have needed that power to stay dry."

Naming our personality barriers empowers us to begin putting into practice a good retirement idea. As we identify, own and claim the barrier, we begin the process of understanding how we can have a degree of control over the power of the blocker.

Second, Honest self-examination is vital for identifying the feelings that have become barriers to accomplishing a good retirement suggestion. This is an important step for limiting the magnitude and power of our barriers.

Examining our insecurities is not an easy task and often uncomfortable, even painful. Leaning into the pain, rather than avoidance, leads to fulfillment in life and retirement. As they say in the world of athletics: "No pain, no gain." As they say in the world of religion: "It is by losing your life that you find it." The pain of self-examination is lessened by the rewards that follow.

A suggestion for your retirement days might be one that does not fit for you. You simply do not want to do it, and self-examination and analysis are unnecessary. Elaine lectures me on the importance of eating healthy and exercising. I am doing better, but I do not want to go as far as she suggests. I have done some self-analysis and concluded her ideas are not for me. Maybe I do not want to admit she is right. I probably have other obstacles, but they seem irrelevant. This does not negate the importance of naming and examining our barriers. The process will open doors for a gratifying retirement.

For the past several months I have had a chronic ache in my back. Recently the ache has become a pain, and my sleep has been affected. I decided to see a doctor.

The doctor examined me and took some tests. When he walked into the room where I was waiting for the report, he sat down and looked me straight in the eye. From the serious look on his face, I knew I was in trouble. Surgery entered my mind. He said in a stern voice, "I have two suggestions for you. First, here is a list of exercises you need to begin. Do them religiously. Second, you need to change your eating habits, both the quality and quantity." He handed me a piece of paper that listed the changes in my diet he thought would make my back healthier.

I responded, "I was hoping you could give me a prescription, you know, a pill that would take care of my back issue." The doctor said, "There is no prescription for your back problem. It calls for a process that will take time, a lifetime." "Are you sure there isn't a good prescription that will help me?" I asked. "No. You need to commit yourself to process which is explained in the two pieces of paper I gave you."

When it comes to our problems, be they physical or emotional, we want the pain to stop. We want someone to tell us the answer and prefer it will not require too much time or energy. We want a prescription. In my judgment, there is not a prescription for having a gratifying retirement. It is a process that takes time, energy, diligence and patience. Most importantly it calls for a process of honest self-examination.

Commitment to a process, rather than having a prescription, is important for achieving a gratifying and healthy retirement. If someone insists on a prescription, there are several excellent books on retirement that offer many suggestions. For example, in his book, *How to Retire Happy, Wild, and Free*, Ernie Zelinski lists approximately 500 suggestions for a successful retirement. These good ideas and others will be difficult to accomplish without self-awareness. Honest self-examination of what may be a barrier to implementing a retirement suggestion is essential to gratifying retirement.

A third step that has helped me with step one and two is asking for assistance from a friend or counselor. I need someone who can be objective. As you enter into the process of self-examination, to avoid wandering aimlessly down this road, draw upon the help available. There are self-help books that will contribute to the process. *After the Honeymoon* gives you specific aids for this task.

The counselor who helped me the most began each session by asking: "What do you want to work on?" For me, the implication of the word, "work" called for serious self-examination. The blocker that may be the most difficult to overcome is having to work at the process of self-examination.

These block/barriers are the theme of the first section of Scott Peck's best-selling book, *The Road Less Traveled*. He writes: "What does a life of total dedication to the truth mean? It means, first of all, a life of continuous and never-ending stringent self-examination."

Harry said to me: "What is the point of all this self-examination stuff. Why make my life more complicated than it is already? If an idea is a good one, just do it. Don't let anything get in your way of applying a positive suggestion to your life."

Positive thinking has its place and is helpful at times. In the retirement workshop that I conduct, I wave a pen in front of a person's face and say; "Don't think about the pen." Then I inflict upon them a degree of pain as I hit them on the head with the pen and say: "Don't think about the pen." They always have difficulty not thinking about the pen.

The "just do it" philosophy and positive thinking are lacking when it comes to dealing with some personality characteristics that keep us from doing what makes sense. There is no substitute for honest self-examination when we want to put into action a good idea.

If you subscribe to the philosophy of positive thinking then "just do it". In my judgment, careful self-evaluation is a key for finding answers that are lasting and fit for you in retirement. Insight into the nature of our individual personality characteristics will enable us to minimize the barriers and integrate a good suggestion our retirement lifestyle.

As you examine your barriers, consider what it means to be successful. I take a hint from the sport of baseball. A baseball player who makes it into the Hall of Fame will fail seven out of ten times. A three hundred batting average is considered excellent.

Leaning to fail is a fundamental aspect of being successful. Throughout my eighteen years of retirement, I have tried many different ways to enjoy my retirement and failed many times. A gratifying retirement happens through accepting failure as normal and part of the process.

Personal power is needed in order to have a gratifying retirement. Activate the emotional and spiritual power that comes from naming the barriers and examining the feelings. The process will be difficult and different. It calls for work and is enjoyable.

# Questions for Personal Reflections and Group Discussion

1. What useful retirement suggestions are difficult for you to implement?
2. What emotional barrier(s) is getting in your way of implementing a good suggestion?
3. How do you respond to the idea of naming and examining the vulnerable parts of your personality?
4. What is your response to a gratifying retirement being the result of a process rather than a prescription?

# Three

## How the Past Influences Retirement

An important ingredient of a gratifying retirement is the desire to examine one's personality and understand how this process impacts retirement.

Beginning at birth, we received messages that live in our minds. These messages form our personality. The messages have a significant bearing on decisions we make on how to live. Many of the messages are healthy and make a positive contribution to our personality and well-being. Some of the messages are responsible for certain unhealthy aspects of our personality.

Early in my career, I was introduced to Transactional Analysis. Throughout my life, TA has helped me understand and examine my personality. TA is a helpful source for naming and examining my emotional barriers for attaining a gratifying retirement.

Transactional Analysis is a theory developed by Eric Berne in the 1950s. Initially trained in psychoanalysis, Berne wanted a method which could be understood and available to everyone. TA puts into understandable and every-day language what I learned in my college psychology classes.

TA talks about three ego states that are part of us: Parent, Adult, Child.

Parent: TA says that we have hundreds of small tape recorders in our head. (If Berne were writing today, in place of "tapes" he might have used DVD or Flash Drive). The messages come from our parents or parent figures, such as older siblings, grandparents, teachers, and neighbors. They may also come from what we learned in church or TV.

The messages on our inner tape recorder occurred at an early age. The parent tapes give children the do's, don'ts, oughts, ought nots, should and should nots. What is right and wrong, good and bad are recorded on our parent tapes. The parent tapes tell us how to respond to a given situation. Some of the messages are nurturing and some are critical. The messages may come to us verbally. Some of the messages are transmitted non-verbally, such as tone of voice, look on the face or a pointed finger.

Child: The child ego state receives the parent messages. These recordings are not filtered or analyzed by a child. They are simply accepted without question. Our internal reaction and feelings form the Child ego state. The Child is the source of our emotions. Sometimes the child part of us responds to the tape messages with feelings of compliance, such as guilt, fear or loneliness. At other times the response is rebellion.

Adult: TA contends that parent tapes are not erased. We can never be completely free from the messages received at an early age. Instead, the adult ego state works to update our tapes with new and accurate information. The adult acts as a computer. It is like a data processing center. The adult deals rationally with situations that are confusing or emotionally unhealthy as a result of a parent message. Our Adult/Computer has the ability to think clearly and determine what makes sense.

TA provides insights into how parts of my personality were blocking me from implementing good retirement suggestions.

While serving my second church, after four years I asked for a three-month leave of absence. I spent the entire summer studying and training at a bi-state mental health hospital and clinic in Ponca City, Oklahoma. I grew professionally and personally during this continuing education opportunity.

One part of the training was my involvement in a "therapy session." There were five other persons in training. Each one had his/her special time when the therapist helped us look closely at our own personality. Through the therapy, I made some changes that enhanced my life, marriage, parenting and subsequently my retirement.

The counselor helped me identify the parent tapes that were responsible for the anxious feelings I had in my work and personal life. He summarized the messages by pointing out that I had a strong "get it right" message.

Two of the suggestions I read in most books on retirement are 1. Adjust to change. 2. Take risks. The "get it right" message erects a barrier for applying these two good suggestions. When my child responds to this message, adjusting to change is difficult and taking risks is threatening.

Updating my Adult Ego State with new and accurate information enhances my ability to adjust to the changes that retirement presents, and take some risks that enrich retirement. The "get it right" tape still plays now and then, but it no longer controls my retirement years.

Here are seven parent tape messages that have the potential for keeping you from a gratifying retirement. I am sure you can add others.

## 1. Be Responsible

We grow up believing that being responsible is good and being irresponsible is bad. The "be responsible" message that plays in our mind is strong. The message can be helpful and healthy. Sometimes, hearing the message "be responsible" leaves us anxious.

We frequently felt the burden of having to be a responsible adult, especially in our employment. We anticipated that retirement meant we would be free the pressure of being responsible. However, freedom from responsibility and the "be responsible" tape message that plays in our mind can be a barrier for enjoying our retirement activities.

The "be responsible" messages are usually accompanied by feelings such as guilt and fear. As a child, if we were not responsible, we frequently were afraid of the consequences. If we were not responsible we heard such words as, "Shame on you," and we felt guilty. These feelings can keep us from enjoying our retirement days.

In retirement, am I being responsible when I play cards, read a book, play with my grandchildren, take a walk, watch TV, fiddle with my computer, play golf and spend time relaxing on my boat? When I am doing these activities, I could easily worry about the fact that I am not being responsible.

A valuable question is: What do I need to do so the "be responsible" tape does not keep me from fully enjoying my retirement? If I do not address the "be responsible" message that I received as a young child, I would easily feel guilty about how I spent my time this week as a retired person.

As you name and examine this parent tape, see whether the following experiences are familiar to you.

Jack: I remember my dad, in no uncertain terms, telling me that if

I didn't start taking responsibility for my behavior, I was going to have difficulty in life.

Jane: I hear my mother saying to me: "Stop complaining. Accept responsibility for what you did. Just get busy doing what you should do and don't blame someone else. Nobody likes a complainer."

Virgil: Dad came into my room when I was a second grader. "Young man; it is time you began taking some responsibility around this house. You are a member of this family and being a responsible person is important in life and in this house. So I want you to start taking responsibility around here, and you can start by keeping your room neat."

Sammy: I can hear my parents saying: "Nobody likes someone who they can't count on. What good is a promise if you don't keep it? If you continue being irresponsible, you're never going to amount to much."

John: I hear my Dad's voice: "You are not going to drive the car until you can prove to me that you are responsible. Lately, I haven't seen evidence of you being responsible."

A friend wrote me and said, "I have been thinking about what you said about the 'be responsible' tape. When I retired I thought not being chained to a schedule and being free of responsibility would be great. I never considered myself a rigid person, but my work provided a degree of structure. I guess I need that. Maybe this is one of the reasons I am having difficulty with retirement. There is almost too much unstructured time that is free of responsibility."

Prior to retirement, every morning you woke up responsibility stared you in the face. Some of the responsibilities were your choice. Many of the responsibilities simply went with the job. In retirement, there are no more deadlines to meet. You can sleep as late as you want. Responsibilities are what you choose, rather than responding to what is pressing.

Examining your "be responsible" tape gives the freedom to decide if and how you are going to be responsible in retirement. Retirement is a time to do what you like. You are free to set your agenda, rather than having it pre-set as the result of work responsibilities. Examining the parent tapes about responsibility is crucial for dealing with what may be blocking you from implementing a good retirement suggestion.

As adults, we associate being irresponsible with children. Adults are more sophisticated and subtle in the way they avoid taking responsibility.

Consider the following statements as evidence. How many times have you said: "That makes me feel," "You make me feel," "She/he makes me feel," or "It makes me feel."

Someone may _make_ you feel pain if they physically hit you. But, no one can _make_ us feel emotional pain. When someone says or does something harmful and hurtful to me, it is not easy to refrain from saying, "They made me feel bad."

Our use of "makes me feel" is our way of not accepting responsibility for how we feel. Taking responsibility for what we feel is crucial for good mental health. No one can _make_ us feel bad. We decide what we are feeling. We choose to feel anxious, guilty, afraid, lonely or angry. We are responsible for how we feel.

Identifying, naming and examining your "be responsible" messages will give you, as an adult, permission to decide how and if you are going to be responsible in your retirement life.

Several years ago a retired friend and I had a conversation about the being responsible issue. A couple of weeks later he phoned me and said; "I appreciate your ideas about being responsible. Lately, I have been feeling irresponsible. I have been doing what I want to do and not being responsible, at least like when I was working. I have looked closely at my "be responsible" tape. Your ideas have given me permission to enjoy my retirement years, do what I want and not feel guilty or irresponsible."

2. Accomplish and Achieve.

These two words are messages that resonate within us, especially in our occupation. When we were working, we received praise and promotions as a result of our achievements and accomplishments. It felt good to be known as a high achiever. When we accomplished a task, we felt worthwhile and useful. We did our best to achieve certain tasks. We wanted to be seen as someone who was proficient at accomplishing what the job required. Yet, many have difficulty with retirement where we are free from the need and pressure to continually achieve and accomplish. We may be disturbed by asking ourselves, "What do I have to show for what I am doing in retirement?"

A person can feel useful and worthwhile in retirement. But, if the accomplish and achieve tape is not named and examined the result may be feeling useless and worthless.

As a child, these words may not have been used, but the message was clear. "Do your best," "Try hard," "Don't waste time."

Trevor has been retired for several years and relates this story. "When I was about seven years old, my Dad came home from work in the middle of the day. I was watching TV. He walked into the room and said, 'How long have you been watching TV? Your mother says you have been lying on that couch all day. I want you to get off your butt and do something worthwhile with your time. You're not going to make something of yourself by continuingly frittering away your time. Retirement affords me lots of leisure time. I hear my Dad's words in my head and sometimes feel guilty when I am doing nothing but enjoying myself."

I woke up this morning, stayed in bed, and relaxed for another twenty minutes. I proceeded to eat breakfast, took a shower, and walked for thirty minutes. I read a chapter in a book, took a nap, went to hit golf balls at the driving range, and practiced my putting. I ate lunch, took a second nap, watched sports on TV, and messed around on the computer. In the evening, I ate supper, played cards and went to bed. What did I accomplish and achieve? The answer: I enjoyed myself. If I play the "accomplish" and "achieve" message in my mind, my enjoyment will be contaminated by guilt.

In retirement, if I am to enjoy my leisure time without guilt, my adult ego state must update the achievement parent tape with new information. I could easily tell myself that I am wasting time because I am not "accomplishing" and "achieving" in the way the parent part of me says I should.

Dan: I have thought lots about what you said about the "accomplishing" parent tape. During my first six months of retirement, I tried hard to do what you suggested, i.e., to name and examine the message in my brain. I thought about how you spend a day and don't feel guilty. I was not very successful in doing that. I guess that is the reason I went back to work halftime."

I reminded Dan that each of us will do retirement in his/her own way. It is not helpful trying to do it like another person. Also, I must confess that I am not guilt-free. It is a work in progress.

Ken: "Throughout my career, people have given me credit for being a high achiever. They are right. When I set my mind to something, I could accomplish it. I guess it goes back to my childhood. Both of my parents were professional people and high achievers. When I retired. I wasn't ready to stop achieving in the way I had before retirement. I have been achieving and accomplishing lots of things, but it has to do with my use of leisure time. I am trying not to feel guilty."

Steve: "You asked me how retirement is going. Actually, I am really enjoying it. But I must admit there are times when I tell myself that I don't deserve to enjoy it so much. I guess I am playing my parent tape too loud and too long. I need to accept that it is okay to enjoy myself and not feel I ought to be accomplishing something."

Retirement is the time in our lives that we do not have enough to do. Many retirees will not acknowledge this reality. Their accomplish/ achieve parent tape is spinning loud and clear. For other retirees, not having enough to do is a perk. Admitting it contributes to the enjoyment of making decisions on what to do with our days.

Many retirees find it difficult to give themselves permission to cease being productive. Throughout our life, people ask, "What do you **do**?" Much of our identity has been tied to work activities. Meaningful work gives us self-worth and dignity. When work is retired, we can easily find ourselves feeling less than fulfilled. Retirement can be experienced as a loss of power, status, and self-worth that we had when we were working.

Retirement calls for us to name and examine how much we need our work identity to be a complete person. Structured work was central to our identity. Our work provided us with a sense of purpose, with expectations, recognition, and rewards. Work afforded us an opportunity to create change, influence and have an impact. Gratification in our work came from recognition, accomplishments, and challenges. It is important to understand how our need to have a sense of accomplishment in our work can be changed into accepting the enjoyment of leisure as an accomplishment. This new attitude will go a long way so guilt will not be a barrier to a gratifying retirement.

3. Don't be lazy.

Am I lazy when I spend an entire day relaxing and enjoying myself? My parent tape says, yes and could easily keep me from enjoying my retirement days. Most of my days could come under the classification of "being lazy." This message will be a barrier for having a satisfying retirement unless I update the tape with new information.

My child ego state says lazy people are weak and unreliable. In retirement, I sometimes feel like a lazy no-good bum when I am enjoying leisure time." My adult ego state has better information that tells me it is okay to relax and do nothing?

Is a mindless activity being lazy? Hopefully, by naming and examining this parent tape, you will not allow the "don't be lazy" message to get in your way of enjoying retirement.

4. The Work Ethic.

In our culture, when someone is known as a hard worker, they receive respect and attention. The work ethic is a drive deeply embedded in our psyche.

John's experience explains how this message can be a barrier for enjoying retirement. "I can remember my Dad saying to me, many times; 'Johnny, get your work done and then you can go out and play.' Both of my parents were hard workers. People would remind me of that fact and say how much they admire my parents. Everyone could depend on them. My parents reminded me of how hard they worked, and that hard work will get you ahead. I grew up with the idea that people who work hard are strong and dependable.

Hard work is intrinsically virtuous and worthy of reward. Most of us have a strong parent tape about the value of hard work. It often determines how people view and know us. For some, hard work is a way to prove their worthiness.

When we were busy making a living, leisure time was viewed as something we earned. If one day, I felt that I did not work hard, I was reluctant to enjoy some leisure. This mentality affects my attitude towards leisure in retirement. Some retirees have difficulty handling substantial leisure time when they are not working hard.

Someone has suggested that in retirement we must learn how to replace the work ethic with the enjoyment ethic. The work ethic message can be a powerful force that prevents some from enjoying retirement. The freedom and opportunity of leisure often bring uneasy guilt feelings.

I have heard many retired folks say, "I am busier in retirement than when I was working full time." Their work ethic message and being busy determines how they feel about themselves. For many, their occupation was a drive to prove their adequacy and worth. In retirement, when we are no longer working full time, sometimes feeling inadequate and unworthy creep into our psychic.

Being busy is a choice. Each of us chooses how we use our time, both in our employment and retirement. Some will say there are professions where the person does not choose how they use their time because the demands on their time are so heavy and consistent. I have been close friends with many physicians, and I know they also choose how they use their time. Yes, sometimes during a day or week a situation was so demanding and critical that it may feel as if we do not have a choice. Everyone chooses if and how they are going to be busy.

In my profession, I heard former pastors brag about how busy they were as if they did not have a choice. There were times when I received an emergency phone call and was asked to come to the hospital. There were times when someone died, and I felt the urgency to respond. Most of the time I decided how I was going to use my time.

When we were working full time, structure and routine was part of the job's expectations and our work ethic. In retirement, we have the freedom to decide if and how we want to structure our days. Retirees create their routine. They decide how busy they want to be. This freedom can be a blessing and also a challenge. For some retirees, this freedom and the work ethic are barriers to deciding the amount of structure and routine they want in retirement. Naming and examining the messages you have about working hard will enhance your retirement days.

5. Don't be selfish and self-centered.

If one adopts the enjoyment ethic, "don't be selfish" and "don't be self-centered" messages need to be named and examined so they will not be a barrier to a gratifying retirement.

Children naturally think a lot about themselves. Both my parents, along with the church, told me that selfishness and self-centeredness are bad. Indeed, many problems, personally and socially, are the result of selfishness and self-centeredness. Being concerned about others is a value to be embraced. I believe that in retirement I can do both. I can enjoy *my* moments and at the same time pay attention to how my selfishness and self-centeredness can impede growth and love.

I have a strong parent tape that comes from my participation in my church's youth group. We had numerous programs on Sunday evenings that taught me the importance of loving and doing for others. I heard sacrificing for others was a Christian attribute. Scripture was quoted to reinforce this message.

In retirement, how I can hold true to this message and still enjoy leisure time when I am doing things for myself? Sacrificing for others is minimal in my retirement days. Determining how I can avoid betraying this truth of living for others, and also live a life enjoying my leisure time is a process most retirees will need to name and examine.

6. Identify what you are passionate about and be the best you can be.

Retirement books emphasize the importance of this message. There are several issues to consider so that this message does not become a barrier to your retirement satisfaction. Your passion may change depending upon your age and health. The degree to which you are passionate about something may also change with time and in retirement.

Thomas spent his life as a salesperson. "I was excellent at what I did. I guess you could say that my verbal skills were my talent. In retirement, I am finding that nobody wants to listen to my sales pitch, let alone listen to me talk. I am not sure I have any other real talent. This is a challenge for me in retirement."

Being the best we can be and fulfilling our passion were vital to being successful in our job. However, some have difficulty incorporating this attitude and spirit into their use of leisure time in retirement. Creating a new and different passion can be a significant retirement challenge. Being the best you can be in leisure time will probably feel significantly different than in your chosen occupation.

7. Be useful. This may be the most formidable tape and is a kissing-cousin of the "don't be lazy" and "don't waste time" tapes.

I visited with a 92-year-old retired school teacher. Rita had a reputation as being an excellent teacher who cared deeply about the emotional and mental health of her students.

Her health was failing. She said, "I am extremely unhappy. I don't know why I am still living. I am ready to die." What should I say to her? My initial reaction was to say something that would alleviate her unhappy feeling. Maybe I should give Rita words of reassurance. Instead, I realized her unhappiness would be a barrier to hearing and implementing any advice or suggestions I would offer. I also knew if I was her age and in such bad health, I might be unhappy.

I decided her unhappiness would be a barrier to anything I might say, including giving her comforting words. Therefore, I invited her to name and examine the unhappy feeling. After a while, Rita finally used the word "useless" to describe what she was feeling. By naming and examining her feeling, I thought Rita was ready to hear some good news.

Rita was a religious person and knew the word Gospel meant good news. I reminded her that God's grace is freely given to each person and is not dependent upon what we achieve or accomplish. I asked her to think about the hundreds and hundreds of children who now, as adults, are emotionally and mentally healthy because of her ministry as a school teacher. In her remaining years, I wanted her to know (and you to know) that being useful is a state of mind that lives within us. It is not dependent upon what we do or don't do with our time as a retired person.

There are probably other messages in your parent ego state that may be keeping you for having a gratifying retirement. These seven parent tapes served us well in our occupation. In retirement, these same messages can be a barrier. Naming and examining these messages is a key for finding fulfillment in retirement. Update these parent messages with new information by activating your informed and intelligent adult ego state.

Most retirees admit having a degree of boredom. Each of these seven parent tapes plays a role in how and why we get bored. Naming and examining these messages enable us to deal effectively with the times when we are bored.

Self-examination is not an easy task. I have found that I needed assistance for the process of identifying my parent tapes and my feelings. I experience help from self-help books, friends, retirement support group, and professional counselors.

Retirement is an opportunity to re-invent ourselves. What is the "new you" going to look like? Naming and examining these parent messages and the feelings that are tied to the messages will ensure that the past will not define the present or the future.

# Questions for Personal Reflection and Group Discussion

1. Has the "be responsible" tape affected your retirement? Why? Why not? What new information would be helpful to put into your adult ego state?

2. Has the "achieve" and "accomplish" tape affected your retirement? Why? Why not?

3. How do you feel about exchanging the work ethnic philosophy for the enjoyment ethic?

4. Do you consider yourself self-centered and selfish in your retirement days?
   Why? Why not?

5. How can you translate into retirement the contributions you made in your occupation?

6. Are you hesitant to examine your personality characteristics? Why? Why not?

# *Four*

Yes, the road to a gratifying retirement varies from person to person. For some, the road is long, with lots of curves. For others, there are detours and ruts along the way. The path will often traverse mountains and go through some valleys. Navigating the road to a gratifying retirement is enhanced through identifying one's unique personality. The purpose of this chapter is to help ensure that your personality contributes to a healthy retirement.

The road to a gratifying retirement is not a destination. It is a journey. Understanding your unique personality will enable you to travel down the road intelligently, patiently and with finesse.

The Myers-Briggs Personality Test is a helpful resource for examining personality characteristics. Marriage counselors have used it to help couples deal with conflicts and grow their married love. Employers have used the test to increase communication among their employees and deal with conflicting situations.

Since 1943 this self-reflection assessment tool has helped many examine their personality type. After these years, it is still a popular and widely used personality-assessment tool, with about 2.5 million tests given each year. Both critics and supporters say that the test endures because it does a good job of pointing up differences between people and offer individuals a revealing glimpse of themselves.

Myers-Briggs theory is an adaptation of the theory of personality traits produced by psychologist Carl Gustav Jung in his 1921 book *Psychological Types*. At the heart of Myers Briggs theory are four personality types.

1. Where we prefer to focus our attention. Where we get our energy, i.e., from within (I) Introvert or from others (E) Extrovert?

2. The kinds of information we prefer to prioritize in decision making— either logical and objective (T) Thinking, or value-based and people-oriented (F) Feeling. Thinking types desire objective truth and logical principles and are natural at deductive reasoning. Feeling types place emphasis on issues and causes that can be personalized while they consider other people's motives.

3. The way we prefer to take in and process information—(S) Sensing or (N) Intuition. Those who are S focus on the present, tangible, and concrete. They prefer to look for details and facts. Those who prefer intuition (N) trust information that is less dependent upon the senses. They are more interested in future possibilities. For them, the meaning is in the underlying theory and principles which are manifested in the data.

4. The preferred style of living and working, either scheduled and organized (J) Judging, or spontaneous and flexible (P) Perceiving. Judging types thrive when information is organized and structured, and they will be motivated to complete assignments in order to gain closure. Perceiving types will flourish in a flexible learning environment in which they are stimulated by new and exciting ideas.

The Myers-Briggs Type Indicator claims that our personality type can be broken down into 16 different categories. For example, my type is INTJ.

People use all of the categories. However, one is generally more dominant and used in a conscious and confident way. From my brief description, you may be able to identify your personality type. Also, the Internet has abundant information to help ascertain a person's personality type and how it impacts his/her life. A shortened version of the test is available on the Internet. Each type could contribute to making retirement gratifying. By the same token, each indicator could contribute to retirement being difficult.

Because retirees have more leisure time, or "downtime" as it was called while working full time, each of us will decide what to do with this new and free time. The quantity of free time in retirement is often is a shock to those of us who spent 40 hours a week or more in our work which was highly structured and provided us with a sense of identity and purpose. This is often a quandary for a retiree. Understanding our personality type will be a significant factor in adjusting to the amount of free time.

If you took the Myers/Briggs test when you were 16 years old, the percent which you tested introvert versus extrovert would likely be different than when you were 30 or 50, and certainly when you are retired. As a teenager, I had many friends and was very social. My occupation called for my extrovert side to be alive and active. In retirement, I find that my introvert nature is preferred and basic to who I really am and manifests itself fully in retirement.

It is my experience that the extrovert/introvert indicator plays a significant role in having a gratifying retirement.

Extroversion-Introversion signifies the source and direction of a person's energy expression. An extrovert's source and direction of energy expression are mainly in the external world --by activities and people. Introverts receive a source of energy primarily in their own internal world—ideas and emotions. Introverts generate ideas for their retirement from within, while extroverts tend to look outside themselves to get ideas.

*The Introvert Advantage*, by Marti Olsen Laney, explains: "Introverts are like a rechargeable battery. They need to stop expending energy and rest to recharge. This is what a less stimulating environment provides for introverts. It restores energy. Extroverts are like solar panels. For extroverts, being alone, or inside, is like living under a heavy cloud cover. Solar panels need the sun to recharge. Extroverts need to be out and about to refuel."

Being an introvert does not imply that you are antisocial, but rather more comfortable with being alone. Introverts may be uncomfortable in large groups and could grow tired of the crowds more quickly than extroverts. Extroverts, of course, prefer the stimulation of crowds and thrive on group activities.

Given that some theories invoke a neurobiological explanation of an extrovert and introvert, scientists have long tried to find experimental evidence for these theories. There have been numerous neuroscience studies conducted on E/I over the years, many of which show that the brains of introverts and extroverts really are different.

Author Marti Olsen Laney devotes an entire chapter to this topic: She writes; "Discovering what neurotransmitters introverts and extroverts use is pivotal because when neurotransmitters are released in the brain, they also engage the autonomic nervous system. This is the system that connects the mind and body and greatly influences our decisions about how we behave and react to our world. I think the link between which neurotransmitters travel what pathways and how they connect with different parts of the autonomic nervous center is the master key to unlocking the temperament puzzle."

Genetics play a role in determining whether we are an extrovert or introvert. Therefore, to ask whether it is better to be an introvert or extrovert is like asking whether it is better to have blue eyes or brown eyes, to be left-handed or right-handed.

If the MBTI test indicates you are an introvert or extrovert this does not mean your behavior is predictable in all circumstances. Although most are either one or the other, a few are ambiverts. They test directly in the middle of the scale. Carl Jung said, "There is no such thing as a pure extrovert or pure introvert. Such a person would be in the lunatic asylum."

When talking about personality traits, psychologists often refer to "optimal levels of arousal." When we are aware of how being an introvert or extrovert influences our lives, we are better prepared to turn what could be a barrier to a gratifying retirement.

It is helpful to resist generalizing. Numerous books on the topic of introverts and extroverts indicate that each has certain definable characteristics. Susan Cain in her popular book, Quiet: *The Power of Introverts in a World That Can't Stop Talking* writes: "Extroverts tend to tackle assignments quickly. They make fast decisions, and are comfortable multitasking and risk-taking…Introverts often work more slowly and deliberately." I know introverts who are risk-takers and make fast decisions. Likewise, I know extroverts who approach some aspects of life slowly and deliberately and can focus on one task at a time.

Some say that introverts are better listeners. I know some introverts who are terrible listeners. Likewise, I know some extroverts who are excellent listeners. There can be a tendency to place labels upon a personality type. Introverts are often seen as aloof, arrogant and insensitive. Extroverts may be perceived as shallow, superficial and insensitive.

The temptation is to point out the advantages and disadvantages of each. The title of the book, The Introvert Advantage" could leave someone with the idea that introverts have an advantage over extroverts. In my judgment, whether being an introvert in retirement is an advantage or disadvantage depends upon how a person accepts and understands their personality type. Often extroverts and introverts responded differently while they were employed than in retirement.

There are several issues for retirees to consider and examine as they decide to make their individual personality trait, extrovert or introvert, an advantage rather than a disadvantage.

Susan Cain spends a significant amount of her book addressing how our culture "sees ourselves as a nation of extroverts. We've been told that to be great is to be bold, to be happy is to be sociable…We live with a value system that I call the Extrovert Ideal—the omnipresent belief that the ideal self is gregarious, alpha, and comfortable in the spotlight." The title of Cain's first chapter is: The Extrovert Ideal. Many in our culture tend to think that becoming more extroverted not only makes us more successful but also makes us better people.

Cain discusses several significant aspects of our society to illustrate how the Extrovert Ideal plays out in schools, workplace, and church.

Cain points to the trend in public schools where the favored method of instruction is cooperative or small group learning. Cain notes that schools and workplaces are designed for extroverts, under the belief that collaboration is key to creativity and productivity (the opposite of which is true for introverts). The theory is that groups produce more and better ideas than individuals working in solitude. From an early age, children tend to be programmed with a message that they will get further in life if you are an extrovert. Natural introverts are often left feeling inferior.

The same idea takes place in the workplace. Team building is elevated and emphasized. The idea is that working together increases communication which results in increased productivity. Cain writes, "A recent survey found that 91 percent of high-level managers believe that teams are the key to success."

Churches talk about the importance of building community and encourage each person to join a group. Church leadership suggests significant things happen in people, and faith is grown through relationships. During the worship, people are urged to stand and greet those around them. All of this leaves the introvert wondering whether he/she has an important place in the church.

Feeling good about being an introvert, and understanding its value, contributes to a retirement filled with purpose and meaning. If not carefully examined, the cultural emphasis on the "Extrovert Ideal" has the potential for introverts feeling they are at a disadvantage.

There is one other challenge for extroverts and introverts that they probably did not face when working. Being an extrovert or introvert becomes more pronounced in retirement.

Another issue for introverts and extroverts to name and examine is the use of time. Early in retirement, not having anything to do feels like a luxury. After a while, so much free time can feel like a burden.

Is being an extrovert and introvert an advantage or disadvantage? Consider the following testimonies.

Randal: "That is an interesting question you asked me. Actually, I never thought much about being an introvert until I retired. Prior to retirement, I welcomed the time I had for leisure. I was just glad to have that time. But in retirement, I have lots of leisure time. I guess being an introvert is working to my advantage since I am okay with having downtime and finding things to do by myself."

Lana:" I am finding that being an introvert in retirement is an adjustment. When I was working fulltime, the social part of my life was right in front of me. I did not have to put much effort into having relationships. But in retirement, if I want to be with people, which I do from time to time, I am finding it requires a degree of effort that I did not have to put forth while working."

Carl: Being an extrovert is working fine for me in retirement. Most of the activities that are offered where I live involve people. I don't have to work very hard at finding relationships.

Karen: Being an extrovert is an asset in the retirement community where I live. Yet, the amount of free time I have is a challenge at finding things to do by myself. All the social activities in which I am involved are great, yet sometimes they are a way to avoid having to deal with the many hours that I am not with people. When I was working, time alone was needed and welcomed. Now I am struggling with all the time I have being by myself.

Leah: You ask whether being an extrovert was an advantage in retirement. I always assumed it was. But I have found that while I was working, friendships were right in front of me. I did not have to think about having a social network, and it certainly did not require much effort. To be honest, I do not have much practice at establishing relationships. Now, in retirement, I am having to work at having a social life. I can do it as an extrovert, but it takes more energy than it did while working.

Another issue for extroverts and introverts to consider is the matter of thinking.

Don: "While I was employed fulltime I did a lot of thinking. I would think about work, family, etc. As an extrovert, I cherished time to think. But in retirement, I find that I have more time to think, and often too much time to think. Sometimes I feel it be would an advantage to be an introvert."

Evelyn: "As an introvert, having time to think was always welcomed when I was employed. But now I have so much time to think as a retired person. I find myself spending time thinking about thinking. I sometimes wonder if it would be an advantage to be an extrovert and not have so much time to think.

Thinking and thinking about thinking can be a positive experience rather than anxiety producing. Naming and examining how much we think and what we think about will ensure our thoughts contribute to a satisfying retirement. Rather than wishing, we could turn off our thinking, we will relax with our many thoughts and enjoy thinking about the past as well as the future. Rather than overthinking, we will play the movies of our mind whereby we harness our thoughts and think about the enjoyable aspects of life.

Because there are perceived advantages and disadvantages of being extrovert or introvert, make sure your personality type enhances your retirement. This happens through accepting who you are as a wonderful gift from God and taking joy in it. Naming and examining your personality will ensure that being an extrovert or introvert works to your advantage.

Throughout my sixteen years of retirement, I have met many people who report that their retirement has been affected by several of the other Myers-Briggs indicators, such as Thinking (T) and Feeling (F).

Thinking/Feeling represents how a person processes information.

Thinking means that a person makes a decision mainly through logic. Feeling means that, as a rule, he or she makes a decision based on emotion, i.e., based on what they feel they should do.

I hope the following stories will be of assistance as you name and examine how your distinct personality impacts your retirement time and decisions.

Ted has been retired for about one year. He said to me, "I know that I am a T on the Myers-Briggs test. That is serving me well in retirement. It is a plus. People get consumed and bogged down on how they feel. I have never been into the feelings thing. For me, feelings just get in the way of clear thinking and cause lots of unnecessary problems. This is the case when it comes to relationships, especially family. I see lots of tension because of how feelings get in the way of rational thought. At the same time, there are members of my family who point out that I am not being helpful when I interject my thoughts into a conversation and avoid the feelings."

Tad has been retired for about four years. He said to me, "I am afraid my T is getting in the way of fully enjoying retirement. So much of retirement time is spent with other people, and in my case, family. Since I have never dealt well with feelings, I only add to the tension when I try to interject rational thought and ideas. Trying to avoid feelings, in myself and others, seems to detract from enjoying retirement. However, I sometimes think a little rational thought needs to be injected into some family situations."

Jane has been retired for about ten years. She said, "I took the Myers-Briggs test several times throughout my lifetime. I am definitely an F. In my opinion, feelings are so very important, especially when it comes to relationships. I don't know how people can avoid their own feelings and the feelings of others. I see lots of problems that are the result of people trying to avoid dealing with feelings."

Fred: I am an F. Sometimes I wish I weren't. I remember in the retirement seminar you pointing out how feelings can be a barrier to implementing a good suggestion. That indeed is true for me. I find myself struggling a little in retirement. Several of my friends have made some suggestions they think would help me. I find my feelings getting in the way of putting into action what they have suggested."

Jack: "I was respected and praised in my job as a guy who could think through an issue or situation, weight the pros and cons and make a decision. I was known as a problem solver and a good one. Many in our office would look to me when they were trying to deal with a complex situation. Yes, there were those who wanted to interject feelings and emotions and, in my judgment, usually distracted from moving forward. Now that I am retired, I am finding that no one wants to hear my thoughts about a situation. Many seem to make decisions about how to use time on the basis of feelings, not rational thought. Since I don't have much practice dealing with feelings and have focused most of my life on rational thought, retirement is a challenge for me. I guess you could say my T is not of much value in retirement."

Bob: "I have always prided myself on being a good student and thinking clearly. I am having some difficulty adjusting to retirement. Sometimes I wonder if the reason is because of my tendency to avoid dealing with my feelings."

So, is it better to be a T or F? The answer lies within each individual. The important thing is to name and examine your T and F in order to tap into your strengths.

Understanding two other Myers-Briggs indicators contributes to a gratifying retirement.

Judging (J) – Perceiving (P), reflects how a person implements the information he or she has processed. Judging is not to be confused with "judgmental" whereby others are evaluated, Judging means that a person organizes life events and, as a rule, sticks to the plans. Judging people think sequentially. They value order and organization. Their lives are scheduled and structured. Judging people seek closure and enjoy completing tasks.

Perceiving means that he or she is inclined to improvise and explore alternative options. Perceivers are adaptable and flexible. They are random thinkers who prefer to keep their options open. They are spontaneous and often juggle several projects at once. They often are known as visionaries.

P's will come up with an idea, and J's will translate the idea into a plan of action.

I am a J. This is both an advantage and a disadvantage in my retirement, especially when it comes to filling up my time. I find it helpful to structure my day. I have certain rituals that contribute to my mental and emotional health. My morning ritual consists of exercise, reading, listening to music, writing, and research on the computer. My J gives me a sense of control over my free time.

Sometimes I recognize how being a P would help with the ever-present need to fill my time. Being more of a P would enable me to be spontaneous and explore the numerous options/ideas for the use of my leisure time.

My friend, Ken, shares his experience. "When I was working fulltime, being organized felt like a requirement for doing the job like it was expected. But with so much free time, a lot more than before I retired, organizing an entire day is nearly impossible, at least for me. I am having to learn how to be more creative and spontaneous with the use of my time. This has not been easy for a J and is an adjustment I am working on."

Susan reports that being a P has served her well in retirement. She explains: "With so much free time, I am able to envision all the options that are before me. I admit that sometimes I feel the need to be more organized with my time. I actually think I need some routine to coincide with my freedom to explore new possibilities. I am working on establishing some rituals. This is helping me adjust to the abundant amount of free time which I was not used to before retiring. Just being aware of how the J and P affect my retirement days has been helpful."

Self-awareness is essential to a gratifying retirement. Discover and enjoy how your unique personality can contribute to a gratifying retirement.

# Questions for Personal Reflection and Group Discussion

1. What are the retirement advantages and disadvantages of being an introvert or extrovert?
2. What are the retirement advantages and disadvantages of being a Thinking or Feeling?
3. What are the retirement advantages and disadvantages of being a Judging or Perceiving?

# Five

## Being Unimportant and Important

In my book, *Death With Style and Grace,* I lift up how to live life and face death with meaning and fulfillment. The same truths are relevant for living retirement with meaning and fulfillment. One central truth is understanding and accepting the paradox: Each of us is important and unimportant.

Over the years, literature, philosophy, and theology frequently communicated truth by the use of paradox. A paradox is a seemingly absurd or self-contradictory statement or proposition that when investigated or explained may prove to be well-founded or true. A paradox may seem like a contradiction, but it turns out to be a resourceful blending of opposites. In a paradox both statements are true, and each has its value. We ponder two truths in a fresh way.

This paradox first hit me at an event that happened with my friend, Mitch. He was a youth director at the 1600 member church I served in Lawrence, Kansas. Shortly after accepting the job of youth director, Mitch began the process to become an ordained elder in the United Methodist Church.

Three years after I retired, Mitch asked me to participate in his ordination ceremony. At the reception afterward, I was standing next to Mitch as people came to greet and congratulate him. Mitch introduced one lady to me by saying: "This is Ms. Cook, She was my favorite Jr. High School teacher." Then Mitch said, "And this is Virgil Brady. He used to be…" and then he paused. I was expecting him to say something like, "He used to be pastor of the church where I worked as a youth director and was a big influenced on my decision to enter the ordained ministry."

Instead, after an awkward pause, he said, "This is Virgil Brady. He used to be (pause) important."

At first, I was offended, but knowing Mitch, I knew he was saying something I needed to hear. I started to think about how I was important as a pastor. Now as a retired person, I was no longer as important, at least in the same way. In fact, I realized that in a real sense, I am unimportant. Naming and examining this aspect the paradox has helped me adjust to retirement.

The road to a gratifying retirement will become smoother as we understand and accept that we are important and unimportant. Each is true and has value.

Contemplate the following information as you consider your importance. There are approximately 3000 visible galaxies. The most distant galaxies are 13.2 billion light-years from Earth. Other galaxies are continually being detected. It is estimated there are 125 billion galaxies in the universe.

I am one of seven billion people living on this tiny planet. Human life, depending on what definition is used for that life, did not arrive on this planet until somewhere between two million and one hundred thousand years ago. Equating the appearance of life on the planet earth to 24 hours, modern human species arrived on the scene about 11:58 p.m. The known history of the world, the establishment of empires, founding of religions, art, music, and science took place in the last two-tenths of a second.

Consider the merits of accepting that we are unimportant.

1. You will resist taking yourself too seriously. This enables you to worry less about trivial matters. You will live by the slogan, "Don't sweat the small stuff." You will be freed from stressing about issues that are inconsequential.

2. Much worry and stress come from being preoccupied with your own welfare. Accepting that you are unimportant frees you from self-centeredness and being self-absorbed.

3. You will keep life in proper perspective. You will be less judgmental and critical. You will be more open to the opinions and ideas of others. You will relax with people and issues that in the past were upsetting.

4.  You will spend less time worrying about what others think of you. You will refrain from trying to live up to others expectations and definition of what is and is not important.
5.  You will not have a need to prove yourself.
6.  You will be more humble which is a positive characteristic for enjoying life.
7.  You will be inclined to live each moment to the fullest, rather than having negative and unproductive thoughts about the past or the future.
8.  Accepting that you are unimportant is not the same as feeling inferior, insignificant and inadequate.
9.  Accepting your unimportance is easier when you also acknowledge that you are important.

Steve spent his career as a physician and responded to my saying we are no longer important in retirement.

"All my life, people were taking and taking from me. I felt pulled in every direction. Yes, I suppose you could say I was important. But I am looking forward to retirement and not being important, not having people making demands of me and expecting me to fix them."

I know what Steve said was true. However, after several years of retirement, I talked with him again. He said, "I have to be honest. I am having a little difficulty being retired." I responded, "Why?" And then I was bold to suggest it might have to do with not feeling important, or at least as important as when he was working full-time. He said, "Maybe you are right. I never really considered being important was that much of a big deal to me?"

A colleague wrote me this testimony. "I have been retired for about ten years. It took five years before I understood and accepted the 'I am not important' philosophy of retirement. I resonated with the title of Harper's book. **I** had difficulty *Stepping Aside*. I did not move on until I began to accept that I was no longer important. I thought that I could not be replaced, at least do the job as well as I did. I didn't realize how much my feelings about myself were wrapped up in my vocation. When I examined my feelings about the fact that I was unimportant, I entered a new and healthier phase of retirement. And I respond well to the 'I am important' part of the paradox. I am important, but in a way that is no longer tied to my professional life. This has given me a new sense of freedom and satisfaction in retirement."

Kay: "Throughout my lifetime, people would frequently ask, "What do you do?" In the retirement community where I live, rarely does anyone ask this question. They often ask, what do you do in retirement? Occasionally, someone finds out about my occupation, and the response is usually one of indifference. It seems as if what I did before retirement is not important. If I am important to them, it has to do with a variety of reasons, but certainly not what I did before retiring."

In our full-time employment, we were important to our employer and fellow workers. The quality and quantity of our work depended upon us realizing our importance to the organization that hired us. To view ourselves as important contributed to the success of our company/business/organization.

For many, a person's identity was wrapped around their career. Yes, you may also have been identified as a wife/husband, daughter/son, father/mother or friend. But, for most of us, our job defined who we were.

Many retirees have difficulty walking away from a life where their self-identity was connected closely with their career. They may no longer feel important. Their self-image may have even been dependent upon what they did in their work.

McKenna speaks to this issue. "Retirement is a hard teacher. It is an ego blow to lose all of the titles by which we have been known for years… Having played a given role for so long, we may lose our personhood to a title…Count on it. Exposure of the naked self comes to all of us when the work ends, the position goes away, and the title gets removed. The proof is on our business card. When it reads nothing but our name, our identity has to stand on its own."

In speaking about retirement, Harper writes: "Simply put, they do not know how to let go. They falsely equate their role with their life and run the risk of defining it in terms of activism, and even worse, by status… Abandonment of their professional role is tantamount to the loss of their personhood."(p.3, 4)

Another way of saying this is that retirement tests our self-esteem.

Retirement exposes how we feel about ourselves. If we had low self-esteem throughout our life, retirement will put this attitude to the test.

Knowing you are important pole of the parodox will be power for embracing the truth that you are unimportant. Your importance becomes even more positive as you affirm that you are important to God.

In your job, your importance was based on what you did, accomplished or achieved. Your importance to God is not based on what you do or don't do, say or don't say. It is based on what is known in religious circles as grace. Your importance to God is unearned, unmerited and undeserved. It is a free gift and frees us to embrace our unimportance.

I am important to my family and a few friends. The central theme of the Scriptures reminds me that I am important to God. We are made in the image of God. (Genesis 1:26) "Therefore, I say to you, do not worry about your life...Is not life more than food and the body more than clothing? Look at the birds of the air, for they neither sow nor reap nor gather into barns: yet God feeds them. Are you not more important than they?" (Matthew 6:25, 26, New Revised Standard Version)

The Bible continually reminds us of God's unconditional and consistent love, no matter how much we mess up. This Truth enables me to preserve a healthy self-image in the face of my unimportance. A positive self-image motivates me to affirm my gifts and use them to make this a better world.

Consider the merits of accepting that you are important.

You will have a positive self-image.

You will not define yourself by what others think.

You will face failure with hope.

You will contribute to the well-being of others.

You will not allow difficult people or situations to get you down.

You will love yourself, i.e., your shape, skin color, sexual orientation, and intelligence.

You will see others also as an important gift from God, thereby deal lovingly with difficult people.

You will be free from the conventional wisdom that defines importance by status, wealth and winning.

You will be better able to acknowledge that you are unimportant.

Lee: Since I retired several years ago, I find that I think more about my own mortality than I did when I was working. For reasons I don't fully understand, this paradox has decreased my anxiety about death.

Someone gave you a book on retirement. There were several good suggestions, but you are having difficulty implementing those suggestions. Understanding, accepting and living the paradox that you are important and unimportant will help activate a good retirement suggestion.

# Questions for Personal Reflection and Group Discussion

1. How can your retirement be enhanced by accepting the idea that you are not important?

2. To what degree is your self-esteem and identity tied to your life before retirement?

3. Do you believe that you are important to God? Why? Why not? How will your belief enhance your retirement days?

# Six

## Time to Prepare for the Big Event

Retirement is a time when thoughts and feelings about death increase. This reality can contribute to a gratifying retirement or become a barrier. Naming and examining our thoughts and feelings about our mortality is an important decision.

Throughout most of our lifetime, thoughts and feelings were focused on activities and responsibilities involving family and work. There was not much time to think about our own mortality. With family and work responsibilities gone or significantly decreased, as a retired person, we find ourselves thinking more about death. We start to feel our age in terms of body image and physical capabilities. We begin to experience the death of loved ones and friends. How much time we have left becomes a real question.

We can deal creatively with our thoughts of death, or we can try to avoid them. Consciously or unconsciously, we tend to push death thoughts away. The natural tendency is to go about our lives and hold our finitude at emotional bay.

Consequently, these emotions work against attaining what we want from retirement. We close off parts of life when we shun thoughts of death. Emotional health begins by facing honestly our tendency to avoid and deny.

I found Judith Viorst's words insightful in her book, *Necessary Losses*. "And our losses include not only our separation and departure from those we love, but our conscious and unconscious losses of romantic dreams, impossible expectations, illusions of freedom and power, illusions of safety and the loss of our own younger self, the self that we thought always would be unwrinkled and invulnerable and immortal…We are utterly powerless… from the inroads of time, from the coming of age, from the coming of death…" Viorst points out that it is through examining our thoughts and feelings about death that we become fully developed human beings. Self-understanding expands the realm of our choices and possibilities.

Some degree of avoidance about death is expected and inevitable. It is normal for people to try avoiding unpleasant experiences. At the same time, avoidance is a major source of unhappiness and fosters dangerous and destructive behavior.

The results of avoidance are the focus of Ernest Becker's Pulitzer Prize-winning book, *The Denial of Death* (1973). This book has been the reference point for examining the personal and cultural consequences of avoidance. Becker says that fear of death ultimately determines all our actions and experiences as individuals and as a society. According to Becker, greed, power, war and wealth have become the modern response in our culture to vulnerability and insecurity in the face of death.

Numerous studies explore how our feelings about death are a significant motivating factor for a variety of experiences in our personal lives. These issues include aggression, stereotyping, need for structure and meaning, sex, self-esteem, marriage, environmental concerns, decision-making, political identity, response to trauma, materialism, greed, prejudice, and of course retirement.

Therefore, the answer lies somewhere between being consumed with thoughts about death and complete avoidance. Retirement is a time when we find a balance so our thoughts and feelings will not be an emotional barrier to having a satisfying retirement.

How does one find that balance? More than likely, my answer to that question will not fit for everyone. My book, *Death with Style and Grace*, offers some suggestions for the process of dealing creatively with the reality of our mortality. In our own way, each person will examine their thoughts and feelings and find a balance that fits for them. For most, it is not an easy task, but necessary for establishing a gratifying retirement.

What is the nature of our avoidance may be the key question? How intense is it? How frequently is it? In what way is our avoidance healthy or unhealthy to our physical, emotional and spiritual health? In some cases, initial short-term avoidance can be a good thing, giving us time to adjust to a painful or stressful issue. It might also be a precursor to making some sort of change in our life. But avoidance has a dark side and tends to be unhealthy.

Becker makes this point: "With denial, we do not get to our authentic self; what we really are without shame, without disguise, without defenses against fear… We shrink from being fully alive."

Retirement can be if we choose, a time to prepare for this all-important event in our lives. In any aspect of life, preparation is the key to success. Our education prepared us for our career. If you want to perform well in a sport, hobby or skill, preparation is essential and increases our chances for success.

A gratifying retirement comes as a result of preparing for the inevitable. The great German poet Rilke said, "Death is terrible only for those who are not prepared for it."

Recently we planned a trip to Europe. Had we not done some preparation, unforeseen events that happened would have ruined our experience. If you are having surgery, you trust the surgeon has prepared. I grew up in Kansas where there were tornados. A city has a warning siren so residents could prepare.

The sixteenth-century Frenchman Michel de Montaigne wrote: "Death is easiest for those who during their lives have given it most thought as though always to be prepared for its imminence." Psalm 90:12: "Teach us to realize the brevity of life, so that we may grow in wisdom." (New Living Translation) Psalm 39:4. "Show me, O Lord, my life's end and the number of my days; let me know how fleeting is my life." (New International Version)

Preparing for our death is neither weird nor morbid. It is an intelligent decision.

How persons prepare for death will vary with each individual. Here are several ways some have prepared. Hopefully, you can add to the list.

1. Death anxiety becomes less intense and frequent when faced head-on. Naming and examining our thoughts and feelings is the first step. Guilt, fear, and lonely are the primary feelings associated with death, although other words may be used for each of these three.

2. Reading authors who address the issue of death helps with the process of naming and examining. This is the primary purpose of my book, *Death with Style and Grace.*
3. Embrace the paradox discussed in the previous chapter.
4. Understand and apply the information in the next chapter.
5. Believe in the Afterlife.
6. Talking with a friend who is comfortable with the topic can be helpful.
7. I have found it helpful to prepare by listening to the witness of people at the time of their death.
8. Prayer
9. Accept the fact that no one can completely prepare for their death.
10. Consider the following positive results that happen when we prepare for the inevitable.

    1. Death anxiety is significantly reduced through the process of naming, claiming and examining our thoughts and feelings.
    2. Contemplating our death stimulates us to live each moment to the fullest. The autumn of life with fewer moments left can motivate us to treasure each moment. We will cherish life's simple pleasures.

In the book, *New Passages,* Gail Sheehy writes: "We need to change the way we measure time and to relax our insistence on control...You want to live each moment as much as you possibly can... If every day is an awakening, you will never grow old. You will just keep growing." Eckhart Tolle in his book, *The Power of Now,* writes: "The quality of your consciousness at the moment is what shapes the future, which, of course, can only be experienced in the Now."

3. We will cherish relationships.
4. We will keep our priorities clear, which includes not taking too seriously inconsequential aspects of life. Status, wealth and success will be put in proper perspective. We will not put off important tasks.
5. We will think more about the things of God and ask the ultimate questions.

6. We will be less concerned about satisfying the expectations of others, especially the unhealthy ones.

7. Our gratitude for life will increase. You can't take it with you. We will focus on making our life count by giving back.

No one can prepare for death if you mean by "prepare" that we will have absolutely no anxiety about dying. I have found that accepting a degree of anxiety about my own death is helpful in my retirement years. The acceptance is freeing and enables me to prepare in a manner that diminishes the amount of my death anxiety.

Thoughts and feelings we have about the end of life is an opportunity to make retirement more gratifying.

# Questions for Personal Reflection and Group Discussion

1. On a scale of 1-10, how well have you come to grips with your own mortality? Why is your number high or low?
2. What has been the most helpful in dealing with your mortality?
3. How do you evaluate the intensity and frequency of your thoughts and feelings about death?
4. What would it take to establish a balance between avoidance and being consumed by your death anxiety?
5. What are the consequences of avoiding thoughts and feelings about death?
6. Why do you agree or disagree with the author's point that thoughts and feelings about death can contribute to a gratifying retirement?

# *Seven*

## Taking Care of the Temple

Are you growing or growing old?

In retirement, there is a slowdown of physical functions and an increase in physical vulnerabilities. It seems as if everything takes longer to do. Thoughts and feelings about aging increase during retirement.

Someone has observed: "Put cotton in your ears and pebbles in your shoes. Pull on rubber gloves. Smear Vaseline over your glasses, and there you have it; instant aging.

Viorst's words offer a positive note to aging. "If we truly mourn the losses of old age, mourning can liberate us, can lead us through to creative freedoms, further development, joy and the ability to embrace life...Age itself may also call forth new strengths and new capabilities that weren't available at previous stages."

There are many resources for helping with the aging process. One of the best is a book by Chris Crowley and Henry S. Lodge, *Younger Next Year*. Here are some of their words that have helped me continue to grow as I grow older.

"The more I looked at the science, the more it became clear that ailments and deterioration are not a normal part of growing old... There is a critical distinction between aging and decay...Aging is inevitable, but it's biologically programmed to be a slow process. Most of what we call aging, and most of what we dread about getting older, is actually decay... Decay is optional, which means that most of functional aging is optional as well... Nature balances growth with decay by setting your body up with an innate tendency toward decay. In the absence of signals to grow, your body and brain decay and you age. What we can do, with surprising ease, is override those default signals, swim against the tide and change decay back into growth."

How do we keep ourselves from decaying? Change the signals we send to our bodies. Four disciplines will transmit healthy signals. Naming and examining these disciplines are crucial so aging will not be an emotional barrier to a gratifying retirement.

Healthy eating

Exercise the body

Exercise the brain

Exercise the spiritual you

Growing up in the church, Bible verses were often quoted to me. One verse that stands out in my mind is I Corinthians 6:19, 20: "Do you not know that your body is a temple of the Holy Spirit within you, which you have from God, and that you are not your own? For you were bought with a price; therefore glorify God in your body." (New Revised Standard Version)

In Biblical days the temple was a sacred place. The Bible reminds us that our bodies are a sacred gift from God. We are admonished to use our bodies to honor God.

If your lifestyle does not reflect a belief that your body is a temple, nothing I can say will convince you. If you see your body as a temple where God lives, these four disciplines are valuable for cherishing and respecting this sacred gift.

1. Healthy Eating

Books, newsletters and the Internet provide a wealth of information on healthy eating. The science of nutrition is developing rapidly. "Experts" do not all agree as to what foods are unhealthy. Make it your job to research how to enhance your health and longevity. Become knowledgeable about what foods can prevent and reverse disease.

There seems to be a consensus about the importance of eating plant-derived foods, fruits, vegetables, whole grains, seeds, nuts, herbs, and spices. The bottom line is what we put into our bodies significantly affects our health and longevity. Simple changes in our diet can impact our health as we grow older.

The book my wife swears by is: *How Not To Die*, by Michael Greger. Dr.Greger pulls together the latest scientific studies on how to fight disease and prolong life. He shows how the right nutrition prevents disease and transforms our genes so we can live healthier and longer.

The book explains that most deaths in the United States are preventable, and related to what we eat. The authors describe what to eat which helps treat the top fifteen causes of death. Diet is the number one cause of premature death and the number one cause of disability.

Greger writes: "For most of the leading causes of death, the science shows that our genes often account for only 10-20 percent of risks at most… It's up to us to make our own decisions as to what to eat, and how to live. Shouldn't we try to make these choices consciously by educating ourselves about the predictable consequences of our actions? Just as we could avoid sugary foods that rot our teeth, we can avoid the saturated fat and cholesterol-laden foods that clog our arteries."

2. The discipline of exercise is an integral dimension a gratifying retirement lifestyle.

Some of life's changes that accompany aging are not under your control, but this one is. Taking charge of your life, physically and emotionally, is the best possible antidote to unhealthy aging. And it all starts with exercise.

I know many people in a wheelchair or confined to a bed who have taken advantage of the many options for exercise in their situation.

As you consider making exercise an integral facet your retirement lifestyle, ponder these words from *Younger Next Year*. Hopefully, you will be stimulated to take care of your temple.

"Some 70 percent of the normal decay associated with aging can be forestalled almost until the end…There is emerging science to prove it…If you don't send signals to grow, decay will win, but even a modest signal to grow, i.e., a decent workout, even a good stiff walk, will drown out the noise…You need to do something every day to tell your body it's springtime…Keep in mind that decay is not biological aging. Decay is the dry rot caused by our modern sedentary lifestyle…Decay can be stopped or radically slowed…Don't think of it as exercise. Think of it as sending a constant 'grow' message to override that crazy tide. Think of it as telling your body to get stronger, more limber, functionally younger, in the only language your body understands…There is only growth or decay, and your body looks to you to choose between them…So exercise is the master signaler, the agent that sets hundreds of chemical cascades in motion… It's what sets off the cycles of strengthening and repair within the muscles and joints. It's the foundation of positive brain chemistry. And it leads directly to the younger life we are promising, with its heightened immune system, its better sleep, its weight loss, insulin regulation, and fat burning; its improved sexuality, its dramatic resistance to heart attack, stroke, hypertension, Alzheimer's disease, arthritis, diabetes, high cholesterol and depression. All that comes from exercise. But if your muscles sit idle decay takes over again…Overall mortality falls with exercise. That is not a surprise when you consider that it is wounded blood vessels that kill you and that exercise heals wounded blood vessels… If you exercise regularly, the chemistry of your blood changes. The fact that exercise reduces death from vascular disease is not a surprise, but how about the fact that cancer mortality falls with exercise and lifestyle as well. Whether the exercise is long, slow, and steady or shorter and more intense is a lot less important than the dailyness of it, six days a week…You absolutely have to understand, endless calories and lack of exercise signal your body that you're heading into a famine that you may well not survive, and in response, your body and brain head into a low-grade form of depression."

The authors back up their thesis with the vast amount of available scientific evidence and offer practical suggestions for exercising and eating healthy. Our bodies crave the daily chemistry of exercise."

I have two barriers that keep me from doing what makes sense when it comes to eating healthy and exercise. First, much of what I enjoy is on the list of unhealthy foods. Second, as I grow older, I find my energy level gets much lower, therefore making it difficult to exercise like I know makes sense. I probably have other reasons (excuses) that I am suppressing. What about you?

3. Exercise your brain

Like our bodies, our brains can start to go downhill as we age, and, while it's uncomfortable to acknowledge, this isn't entirely under our control. Nevertheless, the old adage holds true: Use it or lose it."

There are many things we can do to keep our brains healthy. Older adults report that their memory is not what it used to be. Indeed, there is reliable evidence that memory declines with age, even in persons who are in good health.

For a long time, it was believed that as we aged, the connections in the brain became fixed, and then simply faded. Researchers now believe that following a brain-healthy lifestyle and performing regular, targeted brain exercises can also increase your brain's cognitive reserve. Just as weight workouts add lean muscle to your body and help you retain more muscle in your later years, likewise brain exercises can increase the strength, size, and density of our brain even as we are aging.

Neuroplasticity or brain plasticity is an umbrella term referring to the ability of your brain to reorganize itself, both physically and functionally. Popular neuroscience books have made much in recent years of the possibility that the adult brain is capable of restoring lost function, making it possible to healthily increase the strength, size, and density of our brain even as we are aging. This notion is in contrast to the previous scientific consensus that the brain develops during a critical period in early childhood and then remains relatively unchanged.

The human brain has the amazing ability to reorganize itself by forming new connections between brain cells (neurons). Changes associated with learning occur mostly at the level of connections between neurons. New connections form and the internal structure of the existing synapses changes. Did you know that when you become an expert in a specific domain, the areas in your brain that deal with this type of skill will grow?

Learning new things is one of the best ways to keep your brain healthy. There are ways to give your brain its own workout routine. Studies show that learning something new and complex over a longer period of time is ideal for the aging mind.

Retirement affords us this opportunity. Get your creative juices running and discover what new learning works for your brain. What activity could you begin and/or continue that will stretch and challenge your brain?

4. Exercise the spiritual part of you.

Retirement is an excellent opportunity to grow and strengthen the spiritual dimension of life. Many understand that keeping their spiritual life healthy is the result of maintaining a healthy body and mind. Others exercise their spiritual life through the traditional methods of prayer and reading and studying Scripture. I have a friend for whom guided imagery is her way of praying. Many grow their spiritual life by participating in organized religion where they experience opportunities for worship, small support groups, study, and ministry with and to others. Giving love and personal gifts to a worthwhile cause have enhanced the spiritual life of many. Another person discovered his spiritual life improved when he accepted forgiveness and forgave someone. It is helpful to stay close to those persons who are spiritually strong and growing. This happens through personal relationship and reading their books. (I hope my book will do this for you: *Believe the Believable; Faith in the Face of Diversity*). Knowing our body is a temple where God lives deepens our spiritual life.

Was discipline part of your life prior to retirement? When we were working eight hours a day, keeping in shape was not taken very seriously. In retirement, we have an opportunity to take a portion of those eight hours and get in shape. Every great athlete understands the importance of discipline when it comes to keeping the body in shape. Healthy eating and exercise is a discipline. Keeping ourselves physically, emotionally and spiritually in shape is crucial for having a gratifying retirement.

Because aging is written into the laws of the universe, acceptance of it is a prerequisite for growing older gracefully. Retirement is a great opportunity to make changes in our lifestyle. Most of us have barriers that get in our way of doing what makes sense. This is especially true when it comes to exercising the physical, emotional, mental and spiritual part of us. Naming and examining those barriers are necessary for taking care of the temple.

# Questions for Personal Reflection and Group Discussion

1. What changes in exercising your body, mind, and spirit would add to your retirement years?
2. If you were to make changes, what would they look like?
3. What excuses/reasons/barriers do you have for not taking care of your temple?

# Conclusion

Throughout my life, days and weeks were filled with activities and responsibilities. These tasks came with high expectations. Often it felt as if I did not have a choice. They were an accepted part of my employment and family life. Leisure and free time felt like a luxury.

In retirement, leisure and free time are the new norm. I am free to decide how to fill up my days and weeks. This is wonderful challenge.

One of our children asked me, "Dad, do you ever get bored?" To be honest, there are times I am bored, some days more or less than others. There were times I was bored when I worked fulltime. Most everyone has moments when they are bored. When I get bored, I refer to the ideas in this book. Naming and examining the parts of my personality that initiate boredom helps me move on. I hope you will have the same experience.

When it comes to self-examination most of us need assistance for the process of identifying our parent tapes and feelings. Use the help available from self-help books, friends, retirement support group, and professional counselors.

Final word: Be patient. I have less patience as I grow older. It is helpful to be as patient as possible as you experience retirement. Patience is a crucial ingredient for activating the process that leads to a gratifying retirement. Naming and examining the nature of our personality calls for patience.

Printed in the United States
By Bookmasters